# A Hard Love

Jordan Johnson Kuhn

Copyright 2016 by Jordan Johnson Kuhn

All rights reserved.

ISBN-13: 978-0-9981737-0-2

Author photo © The Studio Sarmiento, 2016

Floating Leaf Press

Printed in the United States of America

*For Daddy*

This book comes straight from my red-clay Georgia girl heart. It was born of a series of memories that have flooded me as I've visited the property that belonged to my paternal grandparents in Montgomery County, Georgia. Lots of tears and love went into the writing of these poems. I hope you enjoy them.

Thank you to Maureen Ryan Griffin, my kindred spirit and writing mentor, for inspiring me so. This book is a product of your light and encouragement. Thanks for helping me to coax my car back onto the highway.

Love to all my Long Pond family. You may find some memories in here as well.

Thanks to my Mama, for smiling down at me while I finished my first little chapbook.

My heart and love and thanks to Erick and Parker for everything, always.

\*\*"Long Pond" first appeared in *Poet's Ink*.

# Contents

## PART I: Innocence

The Photograph ............................................................ 13
Rope Swing .................................................................. 14
All the Food I Wouldn't Eat ......................................... 15
Red Apples ................................................................... 16
Beds, Part I .................................................................. 18
Song, Interrupted ......................................................... 20
The Laundry Room ...................................................... 21
Heels ............................................................................ 22
Grizzle ......................................................................... 23
Community House ....................................................... 24

## PART II: The End of the Beginning

Careful Boundaries ...................................................... 27
Ghostly ........................................................................ 28
The Garden .................................................................. 30
First Death ................................................................... 32
Clothes on the Line ..................................................... 33
Clippings ..................................................................... 34
The Fire and the Flood ................................................ 36
A Birthday Wish .......................................................... 38
The Diamond ............................................................... 40

## PART III: Absolution

Long Pond ................................................................... 43
Learning to Fly ............................................................ 45
Beds, Part II ................................................................. 47
Repose ......................................................................... 48
We Were There at the Last .......................................... 49
The Procession ............................................................ 51
Gifts Never Received .................................................. 53

Infant Daughter .................................................................. 54
The Sharecropper's Cabin ................................................ 55
The Love that Remains ..................................................... 57

## Epilogue

Praise Poem ....................................................................... 61

# Innocence

## The Photograph

A yellowed picture of
    a couple with a baby,
        me, newly minted, so tiny.

The couple is thin, young, shiny.
    He is dark, and she is fair
        and they have made this baby.

She holds me, close, on the rocking chair
    while he crouches beside us, smiling,
        and it is my first visit here.

The picture stood in the living room for years,
    even after we three no longer posed together,
        my mom's smile etched lovingly, centered.

There was no way to tell, from this snapshot,
    that we would not wander through life together.
        Divorce and death, illness

and lack of understanding, the fingers
    of the darkness that can happen, had not yet
        stroked us, had not yet played their part.

## Rope Swing

Once (I was
young) upon a time,
my grandfather was alive
and he made a swing so long
I thought my toes might touch the sweet sunshine
and my Daddy sang that I was his
Sunshine and the world
was lovely and
blue and
yellow
once.

## All the Food I Wouldn't Eat

She cooked for days—
cornbread, flattened like a pancake,
green beans with ham, creamed corn from the garden,
peas, always peas,
snapped and shelled by hand. *I still remember
her hands,
the only pudge on her
the skin between
her thumb and her wrist, snapping
those peas, shell by shell,
bits of them falling.*
Okra, fried in the grease,
innumerable vegetables, unfathomable
to an eight-year-old who ate
nothing green.

On Thanksgiving, as always,
we held hands, we gave thanks.
Blessed the food. And I ate maybe
a piece of ham and a bit of a roll.

And after all those days of choosing,
and cooking, and shelling, and peeling,
she would wait
a moment, then rise
quietly from the table, pat my head,
and return with a peanut butter sandwich.
My Thanksgiving.

And I would feel her *I love you,*
without any need
to hear it.

## Red Apples

My green, cane-woven kitchen chair
faced the painting
of the red apples, the one
I stared at, transfixed,
every time I picked at my food
on our trips to my grandparents' house.

Painted by our cousin Gail,
a most gifted artist—
her yard full of sculptures,
her house full of wonder—
it found its way here, somehow.
Just down the road.

As I grew, so did
my love of the apples.

At first, I loved the way
they were red
and shiny; my vocabulary
was small, and I was small,
and I could have eaten them up,
could have gobbled the paint.

As a teenager, I took painting classes,
and looked at them again, turned a deaf ear
to supper conversation,
staring—

*How did she make them so round?*
*With the shine in the perfect place,*

*so that I could even tell
where the unseen light fell upon them?
How did she mix those colors—just so—
to get that red?*

For years and years,
out here, lost somewhere in the hush
of the South Georgia heat,
and rain, and moonlight,
there hung upon a wall
a quiet, painted canvas
of perfectly red, perfectly round,
perfectly apple-y apples.

The yellow wallpaper of the kitchen
is faded now, a big rectangular fade,
strips of sun-beaten,
humidity-eaten paper spiraling
themselves off the wall in defeat

in the spot where the apples,
perfect for such a brief time,
were just apples.

## Beds, Part I

I think of the South Georgia rain—
the way it must have sounded on the rooftop

to two boys, inches apart on their twin beds.
It must have trickled down the windows,

perhaps lulling them into sleep,
to dream of football, or girls, or

of the work they had to do.
Those two pine beds

with the white knit bedspreads. . .
There was a guest room, too, reserved

for rare guests, but it may have been better
for them to have been separated instead.

Did they whisper across the little aisle,
over the green shag carpeting?

Or did they turn their backs, each one
dreaming separate dreams?

There was a mirror to reflect them—did they
slick back their hair with pomade? Button their shirts?

Check their pimples? Did they iron their pants?
(More likely Mother did it for them.)

I found varsity letters there, faded
notebooks, a Charlie Brown figurine,

a certificate for the Children of the Confederacy,
stuffed back into one of the drawers.

There was a gun rack on the white clapboard wall
and a brass lamp on a nightstand between the beds.

Who went to bed first? Which one sighed in his
sleep? Who stayed up reading by the weak light?

As the years slid by, was their conversation easy?
Did they love each other then?

## Song, Interrupted

She would sing in the kitchen,
the old hymns, the ones
they don't sing anymore.

She hummed, too,
daydreaming, wiping dishes
while staring out the window
at the highway.

I would sneak up behind her
this foot *here*,
this foot *there*,
*ever* so quietly
and then yell *BOO!*

She would throw her hands
up in the air,
and say *MY LANDS!*
(there was no cursing
in this house), the suds flying,
a plate clattering,
sometimes to the floor.

But she would laugh,
and shake her finger,
and pick up her plate,

then make me a tray
of thumbprint cookies,
or a peanut butter sandwich
with the jelly mixed in.

## The Laundry Room

A catch-all, they sometimes called it—
a sunny room at the front of the house.
My grandmother worked here,
washing, polishing. Shining linoleum,
a farmhouse sink—appropriate.
A rusted icebox, full of green-bottle "Co-Colas"
that she would open (the bottle cap bursting off
the top) and hand to me
with sudsy hands. *Not too much, now.*

I loved the cabinets, filled with the old
and the practical things.
Mason jars, folded-up papers,
what seemed like hundreds of grocery bags,
ancient baskets and vases,
a homemade butter-maker.

The room held flowers
and sunlight—the presence of a woman
who swept here, heels clattering on the floor,
who ran the water through the sink,
the hard *swoosh* a satisfying sound.
The window faced the highway.
As she shelled peas, and washed and sang,
did she see the cars fly by?
Did she wonder what else the world held?

## Heels

I never
remember
a time when she
didn't wear her heels.
Her ankles would swell, and
doctors would warn her of falling,
but      she was a lady. And ladies,
even          around the house, wore heels.

## Grizzle

He always had a pen in his pocket, my grandfather.
It was impossible to press up against him,
to be cuddled. The pen always poked, painful,
and his eternal five o'clock shadow was rough.

On the rare occasions I touched his face,
or when his cheek brushed mine,
I instinctively recoiled,
the bristles chafing my skin.

Was he as hard a man, as tight-lipped
as he seemed to me?

I reach back, ashamed,
for the memory of a moment
when he wanted to give me ten dollars
to take shopping.

I was too scared of him. I didn't want
to go back in, didn't want to take
his money, so I held my cousin's hand
and climbed into the car.

## Community House

The community house—*a lovely phrase for a place that houses the community*—stands small and white and smells the way you think the 1950s must have smelled. The annual family reunions happen here, events that require nametags, and always people gone and people born by the time the first weekend in May rolls around again. You come maybe once every five years, and when you do you are embarrassed that you do not know many of their names. *You once introduced yourself to someone you thought a stranger, and he informed you that he was your uncle.* But that stops mattering when it's time for the food—a long, long, endless table of Southern nourishment. It takes you ten minutes to get through the line and then you need to go to the cooler and get your sweet tea and then so many people want to tell you that they haven't seen you since you were *this big* and you sure look just like your mama.

# The End of
# the Beginning

## Careful Boundaries

*after Lisel Mueller's "Necessities"*

They had careful boundaries, my grandparents.
He a farmer, a saw miller, a tax commissioner,
she a worker for the Welfare Department,
always busy with something in her hands at home.

There were boundaries of time—
one did not sleep late in the morning.
There were boundaries of place—
the thought of life as an open road did not belong.

And there were certain spots one simply did not go.
There were boundaries of speech—
some set in place by the stoicism of tradition.
One did not necessarily need to express affection.

But there were the moments when
        boundaries were broken,
when my grandmother let my lazy self
        slumber until noon.
When my grandfather reached out
        to me with a seldom-seen smile,
            rendering me unafraid.
When my grandmother dropped a pot,
        not knowing I was nearby, and said
*Oh damn—*

        these were my favorite times.

## Ghostly

Ghosts walked over yellow linoleum.
    I was certain.

          I would lie on the old bed in the
white clapboard room in my grandparents' house,
   the rose branches
tick-ticking on the window,
     the utility light in the yard
the only glow for miles.

I always imagined silvery
      figures
dancing in the dew-dampened fields,
         gliding
   over the rows of vegetables until dawn.

Our family's old plantation house down the road
    was most definitely haunted—I could see
fingertips
    in the old lace curtains, hear strange
    sounds
though the cupboards were silent.

Those were not my ghosts. I shied away,
    feeling the house push me away,
        back to my grandfather's home.

In the mornings, the ghosts disappeared. But,
after my grandfather died, I
   heard a story that someone rummaging
in the refrigerator looked up

and saw him walk slowly
    across the kitchen.

Sleeping in his house, I would squeeze
    my eyes tightly shut,
lying in patterns of moonlight, hearing squeaks
and scratches.

Funny now, though, as I sift
    through old dance cards,
unopened gifts in faded
tissue, as I sneeze from the dust,
    I keep looking up at dancing
        shadows, at sunlight slanting
through the glass.

And I hope to catch a glimpse of him—
    to say goodbye again.
        To say hello.
            To say I love you.

## The Garden

She was from the old South, a lady
   who wore a khaki skirt and a proper sunhat
     as she worked in the garden.

The farm was just a farm, full
   of rows of green, growing things
     that did not interest me.

But the garden was different.
   She would let me hoe, all
     the colors of the flowers

swirling around me, the sunflowers
   almost taller than me,
     as I hacked away,

and she wouldn't mind
   that I didn't know how to hoe,
     missed the weeds and ruined the flowers.

There is an old photo
   of my cousin hugging me
     in the garden.

Here, it was easy to love,
   in this little plot of flowers
     spilling onto the driveway.

It was so orderly,
   the buds all in line, a controlled
     cacophony of color.

And now it is gone,
    overgrown and rotted,
        the footprints of the ones who worked here

erased or buried underneath
    a tangle of weeds, the ones
        I used to battle—they won at last.

## First Death

The first time you hear about death,
you are little, an innocent. Your stepfather
tells you not to play that afternoon, to wait
for your mother so that she can come home
to hold you as she tells you.

You do not understand.
You haven't yet met death, you don't realize
in your world of sand and sunshine that it waits,
ominous, at the end of the tree-lined
country road, for all of us.

You head south, the dark blue dress
your mother buys you wrapped carefully
in your suitcase, lest it wrinkle,
you don't want it to be wrinkled
for the funeral of your grandfather.

You arrive at the house, and it is quiet, and his chair is
empty.
People come and go, and there is food,
and you do not understand.

Someone takes a photo at his funeral, of the coffin,
and in the photo, you can see his face.
You wonder
why someone would take such a picture.

And it rains as they lower him into the ground.
And there is a great rustling, you feel it as you stand in
your blue dress,
in the rain, not understanding.

## Clothes on the Line

Hidden, stretched out in the backyard,
where I almost never went alone,

was her green clothesline.
She was the only person I knew

who still hung clothes out to dry,
bleached by the sun, on hot summer days.

I would watch as she pinned the sheets,
pinched them carefully.

But they would still billow in the breeze
as I danced in and out.

## Clippings

The newspaper was a big deal.
She would read it with an occasional *mm-hmm*,
nodding or shaking her head, reading aloud
the particularly juicy tidbits.

Someone was getting married, or had gotten engaged
but had broken off the engagement after the
newspaper ran.

The Garden Club would meet on this day,
she would see, and she would carefully
cut that item out, smoothing the paper
with her busy hands.

When I was a little speller and went to Washington
for the bee, the occasion somehow crept its way into
that small-town paper,
and she clipped it out,
saved it in a box long past the time
it turned yellow
and curled at the edges.

Often, when I awoke down here,
the first sounds
that I would hear
were the rustle
of the newspaper
and the creak
of the rocking chair in the living room,
accompanied by
the scent of frying bacon.

And it comforted me to know
that she was rocking in her chair
as I rose from sleep,
had been keeping watch,
reading the paper.

### The Fire and the Flood

After dinner, Daddy liked
to drive alone
down the dusty roads.
I stayed behind, helping
my grandmother weed the flower beds.

Once, she was showing me
how to pull up
the green shoots, making sure to destroy
the roots, when I glanced up
and saw the flames.

It took me a moment; I was fascinated
by the orange fingers
on the curtains, strangely beautiful,
as they danced over
each other, ascending.

I pulled her sleeve, pointed,
and she yelled *Fire!*
Summoning my grandfather, moving
toward the house, telling me *Stay put*,
all in one slow-fast second.

A young girl, pale
and alone, trembling
in the yard, the shock made absurd
when Daddy drove by, honking,
unaware of emergency.

The dark smoke began pouring its way
out of the white windows, devilish,
the black and orange the only
colors that mattered now,
the summer-green gone.

After a series of hisses, a flood of water
to quench the conflagration,
my grandparents emerged, soaked,
both triumphant and defeated.
Daddy arrived home to the tale

of a pot of grease left to its own devices.
Years later, it haunts me, this memory
of a fight to save a house
so loved, which would one day
surrender anyway.

## A Birthday Wish

It was her birthday, her ninety-first.
It would be the last.

We gathered together, the ones
who were left, threw her a party.
She wore one of her dress-up dresses and a big
corsage, and heels. Always heels.

It seemed odd, this family reunion
in December. Reunions
were held in late spring, the heat
already sweltering.

As the children played in the yard
that day, though, the trees were bare,
a last litter of leaves
crushing under their feet.

As always, I had somewhere to go,
somewhere to be, speeding
back to Atlanta
as soon as I could steal away.

She was safely ensconced
in her rocking chair,
guests bending down to wish her well,
talking loudly so she could hear.

I wish now that I had lingered,
had knelt by the chair
and held her hand longer.
*She always gave my hand a squeeze when I held hers.*

I might have stroked her hair, gently, but she would
have pushed me away.
That would have been too intimate,
too close.

I wish I could remember
what I gave her,
though I'm sure my gift
went unused.

I wish I had known.

## The Diamond

After thirty years of bidding premature adieus,
guilting us when we left—
*I hope I'm still around next time you visit*—
she knew when the real time was nigh.

The morning of her birthday celebration—
the one that would be her last—
she took off her diamond solitaire,
the gold worn thin
from decades of constant wear,
pulled me aside, and pushed it, hard,
into my hand.

*It was mine*, she was saying.
*Now it is yours.*

I was startled by the gift,
by the suddenness of this everyday-sacred
ring being thrust into my palm.

*I remember the times when she would bake,*
*the dough rising, her rings*
*laid on the nearby counter.*
*I remember that the solitaire never quite*
*seemed to fit on her finger,*
*that she would turn it around and around*
*when she talked.*

I thanked her, the tears coming,
and she squeezed my hand,
padded off to get ready for her party.

# Absolution

# Long Pond

The inevitable disrepair—
I see it as I walk, ruminant, among fallen pines,
crunching straw, crackling the day.
Each time I come here,
things seem more grey.
There are new wrinkles, creasing her skin
like thread through butter.
Her mind, though, is still sharp,
as is her tongue.
She is old now, harsh, able to love
but not to show it.

I walk back, near the barn, rusted silent,
gaping at me, openmouthed. I fear it
and do not venture closer.

I touch the brittle vines, intertwined corpses,
planted long ago by fingers whose work
has now ceased,
and wonder if he ever made wine
from these few grapes,
wonder if their taste held the hard sunshine.

This was a world of my childhood.
She would sing hymns, bake cookies,
read aloud from clippings and lather her hands.
He was always in the fields.
There were sunflowers, and butterflies
that would alight if I stopped moving
and stood stock-still.

There was sweet tea and watermelon—
baking sun, peppermint, fierce red ants that bit my
feet if I stepped child-carelessly.

Now the fields lie fallow, and I have grown.
She can barely walk and there are only brief visits.

He rests in the ground and I visit before I go,
wonder what it would be like to slumber here—
so parched one season and bone-cold the next.

Such a silence, such profound stillness—
the permanence of the hard-packed red clay.

I say my goodbyes,
and we honk the horn twice.

## Learning to Fly

When I was little, I would sit on my Daddy's lap,
my paws on the steering wheel,
guiding the car, passing others.
We would count the cars
on the highway, yelling *Popeye!*
at the ones with only one headlight.

It was a boat, that white Buick Riviera
of my Daddy's. Driving it, like navigating a yacht
down the dusty country roads,
the tires crunching the sand and gravel, occasionally
sliding sideways if I attacked
a bend in the road too fast.

Daddy let me drive down here,
before I had the legal plastic to do so.
The highway was empty,
and I could roam,
feeling so grown-up as I accelerated,
clouds of red dust swirling
behind me, disturbing the peace.

It hit me once, somewhere
on one of those old back roads,
that perhaps I should not fly.
Perhaps I should drive more slowly,
windows down, radio off,
listen to the fields, savor the stillness
and loveliness of the unpaved road.

I drove along the sandy roads,
past the murky swamp,
down by the old highway,
turned around, went back
to the house. And my Daddy
was there, waiting to hug me hello,
as I handed him the keys.

## Beds, Part II

    I never remember my grandparents sleeping
                  in the same bed.
      Their bedroom had two big beds,

hers on this side                        his on this.

    They were never affectionate with each other.
    But his last word, before he died, was her name.
And I found out later that, in the deep of the night,
       when the only sounds were far-off
      trucks rushing down the dark highway,
    they would hold hands across their tiny aisle.

# Repose

Way back, past the old highway, tucked
behind all the bends in the road,
in the shade, in the silence,
there lies an ancient graveyard.

You have to park and get out of the car,
approaching carefully, to find it.
It is tiny, the lichen and creeping decay
edging out the letters on the gravestones.

They slumber here, these early settlers,
steeped in the stillness,
the location of their resting
places known only to a few.

I wonder, as always, how my ancestors
can feel so far away, so separate,
yet so close and so much a part of me,
at the same time—

I can still hear their breath, their thoughts.
I can picture the way their hands
must have looked, calloused, farmers' hands.
They built their own place

in the world, found their way somehow
to this quiet corner of the South
to plant roots, to raise children, to worship.
To find a place to lay their bones.

## We Were There at the Last

A call came, a summons.
It was time for me to leave, to travel south,
thinking of farewell words
as I watched the white lines on the highway.

She was so small.
The hospital bed shrunk her
so that she looked less herself,
more like a body that could be anyone's.

Wires and tubes coiled,
callous things, snaking their way
around the bed, around her
shoulders, around her stilled hands.

I picked up one hand, gently, so gently,
gave it a squeeze like I always did.
She did not squeeze back.
She did not move.

Daddy said it was not going to be now,
so I left, hunched over,
somehow wearing the weight
of my childhood on my back.

But I was called back a few minutes later.
And she had gone.
Had taken her leave like
good Southern ladies do.

She had waited for me,
and I held her hand again,

there at the end of the beginning,
the last of the goodbyes.

## The Procession

We gather at the plantation house—
Spanish moss on trees, a lost vestige
of the Old South—the South we speak of rarely.

We are here to honor her,
to walk across the road into
the old church, where her body lies.

I stand in this crowd, this crowd of people I know
and I don't. The same blood runs in all our veins,
as the others wait across the road,

at the church that is Baptist
one Sunday and Methodist
the other, because this place is so small.

It is a glory-day,
a September full-sky day.
It doesn't feel like a funeral day.

We mill about, unsure—who will give the signal?
Who will lead?
A police car pulls up, and we silence.

Someone gives an unseen sign,
an officer throws up his hand,
and we shuffle, dutiful, across the tread

of a well-worn rural highway.
The only vehicles that have to stop are trucks,
long-haulers who fly down this quiet road.

My boyfriend, bred a Yankee,
stands at my side, taking in this tradition
that seems so strange to him.

It seems strange to me,
yet somehow familiar,
as I have known all along that I would be here,

one day, in this place, saying goodbye
to my grandmother I knew, and I didn't know,
who somehow is so much a part of me.

We file into the church, shushed,
and one cousin speaks of her strength.
Another speaks of her softness.

She is laid in the ground,
and then we shuffle back across the road,
numbed, to eat fried chicken and be comforted.

# Gifts Never Received

We would give her gifts, my grandmother—
a housedress for Mother's Day,
a brooch for her birthday—
she would thank us
but they would lie unopened,
tucked away in their appropriate places
(the china cabinet, the guest closet)
objects still wrapped in tissue and forgotten.
As I help clean, this very final cleaning,
this emptying-out, I discover gifts,
some with tags still on them,
crisp, fresh, and I wonder *why?*

What held her back from en*joy*ment,
from holding things in her hands that would
bring her joy? Was she too stubborn?
Were her hands clasped so tightly
that she could not open them
for the grace of reception?

Was she afraid? Was she scared
to use these beautiful, new gifts
because if she used them up,
there might be no more?

On our drive home,
with the lights of the highway blinking
like seconds ticking off the clock,
I touch my husband's hand
and tell him that, starting tomorrow,
we will use our good china.
But we don't.

## Infant Daughter

I didn't know she existed—
and she only existed for maybe a few hours,
maybe less; they never spoke of her—
I didn't know she existed
until I grew old enough to read the gravestones.
They never gave her a name.

I imagine her running through the fields,
hands outstretched, brushing the corn,
hiding among the stalks.
Maybe she wore a pink dress,
maybe it had a smear of red clay on the hem.
Maybe the skirt twirled.

I never realized the significance of not naming her—
the pain she must have caused when she arrived,
and then didn't—
how they wouldn't have wanted to name
that pain, to give it a title.
To make her real.

And many moons later,
my daddy wanted a daughter,
to give his mother a girl.
And many moons later,
my son was born. On the birth day—
and death day—of Infant Girl.

But he stayed. And he took
his grandmother's maiden name.
He took the name that might have gone
to another. And he stayed.

## The Sharecropper's Cabin

We wait for my dad to arrive—my husband and me,
walking through the fallow fields,
swatting gnats, swearing softly when one triumphs.

I take a phone-snap photo of the old red barn,
a beauty from a distance,
and of a butterfly flirting with the barbed-wire fence.

My husband braves the overgrown ditch down
the gravel-sand road, jumps onto the bank
to explore the old cabin.

I am too afraid to make this leap,
so I shuffle along the road, hands in pockets,
looking up at the sky, waiting for the rain.

As a young girl, too, I was afraid
of this place, of these fields.
I imagined that ghosts danced here,

gliding noiselessly over the rows,
coming ever closer to the main house,
their fingers raking through the clay.

Now there is a different fear, a real foreboding.
I am here for the first time without my father;
I do not want to be here without him.

And the house I used to run back to
is falling apart in disgraceful decline—
the wallpaper peels off the boards, ghostly itself,

giving up, flaking back toward the earth.
The roof, too, is caving in,
and there is nothing I can do to stop it.

I take it all in, take deep breaths, take in the land
and the earth, and turn back toward the main house
as my husband clatters in the sharecropper's cabin.

Later, he will tell me about the dismantled phonograph
in the corner, a porch slanted almost into the ground.
But I already realize the finality of this. Of all things.

## The Love that Remains

To be honest, I mostly hated
going down there when I was a kid,
hated the gnats, the heat, the smell of the aging house.

I hated the way my grandparents were so distant,
so unlike my other grandparents,
who were funny and loving, who kissed and hugged.

Mama Johnson was birdlike, grabbing me
from corners, sometimes startling me.
Pa would try to wrap me in an occasional hug,

my body writhing away from the pens in his pocket
and the stubble on his chin, so rough,
the experience always so poky and uncomfortable.

But now, grown into adulthood,
eyes widened and saddened by loss upon loss,
I view the old house, empty and overgrown,

as a love song.
As the only love song possible
in that latitude, that longitude.

There was anger there,
a smoldering anger, never spoken aloud.
But there was also love.

And love is what remains.
The love of a mother for her children,
two grown to adulthood, one in a tiny grave.

The love of a grandfather for his grandchildren,
nicotine-scented hands caring
for them as best he could.

The love that was shown
through work, through the
hardest, most calloused work.

And there was love that was born there,
the love my father carried for me, always,
the love that triumphed,

despite the years he must
have felt unloved.
The love that remains.

# Epilogue

## Praise Poem

*after Barbara Crooker's "Praise Song"*

Praise the memories the follow me down
this old, battered highway.
Praise the way they have fallen,
layering themselves upon my life.

Praise the two souls who joined together
so long ago, without whom I would not be.
Praise the magnolias, the pecan trees, the plants
and flowers that have graced this Southern ground.

Praise the old garden where she once stood, coaxing
beauty and color out of the earth.
Praise the fields where he once worked, bringing
life and nourishment into the world with his hands.

Praise the old bell, which once rang
to call two boys
in from the fields for dinner,
to be fed, to rest.

Praise the occasions that were celebrated here,
the birthdays with their showers
of gifts, the joining of hands
in November at a groaning table.

Praise the love that lived here,
in whatever form it took.
Praise the blessings it brought
to us and to others.

www.ingramcontent.com/pod-product-compliance
Lightning Source LLC
Chambersburg PA
CBHW032058040426
**42449CB00007B/1121**